Sparrows at the Breakfast Table

Richard Douglas Pennant

Illustrated by Yiannis Douglas Pennant

Published by Cinnamon Press
Office 49019, PO Box 15113, Birmingham B2 2NJ
www.cinnamonpress.com

Print Edition ISBN 978-1-78864-157-9

British Library Cataloguing in Publication Data. A CIP record for this book can be obtained from the British Library.

Cinnamon Press is represented by Inpress.

Designed and typeset in Adobe Caslon Pro by Cinnamon Press.

Acknowledgments

With thanks to Jan and Adam at Cinnamon Press for their editorship, cover design, and creative mentoring.

Richard Douglas Pennant

North Wales born in 1955, Richard Douglas Pennant is very proud of his ancient Celtic roots and heritage. Educated at a variety of schools he also attended two eccentric crammers, one situated for a time in the wing of a castle in the north of Scotland and the other in a converted windmill on the South Sussex coast. He has worked in the independent welfare sector. Seafarers' welfare work took him to—among other places—the Ports of Rotterdam and Singapore in the early 1970s and later he worked with the homeless in Middlesbrough. A man of wide interests, of which writing is one of his passions, he also enjoys drawing, researching ancient history, spiritual philosophy, and (curiously) oilfield history and archaeology. He regularly tours performances of his work with fellow poets and jazz musicians. He has studied under poet and author Ian Gregson and actor and theatre director Robert Bowman. Richard Douglas Pennant is married with two grown up children and shares his time between homes in North Wales and Cyprus.

CONTENTS

To Richard Polo and Aiden
with an abundance
of love and appreciation.

Pappous.

Do not grow old,
no matter how long you live.
Never cease to stand like curious children
before the Great Mystery
into which we were born

Albert Einstein

Sparrows at the Breakfast Table

Bel and the Dragon

Big

isn't a word big enough,

Huge

still doesn't do the animal justice;

E-n-o-r-m-o-u-s

now we're getting a little closer,
but still way off the mark.

Size

is everything;
and its that which makes this creature so fearsome. I mean that
monstrous head and mouth filled to the brim with teeth, each one of
which is a megalith large enough to stop a tank in its tracks… but no
forked tongue, that is something our worst nightmares bestow upon
politicians

… venom!

But there again, have you
ever seen size so lithe,
grace to match its swim
through air… slender-
bender? On wings that
could lift Noah and his
Ark fully pay-loaded—so
strong, but lace dainty,
they're the barest gossamer that sieves the light and cloud shadow

… how the creature owns the sky.

Smoke and flame?
Not a breath in the still air,
who needs the Catherine Wheel when you've got flight like this. And the
roar? That's just distant squall taking shelter under thunder.

And hanging onto its neck, slender as a plesiosaurus's, the small hands of
a child, palm down, balance the boy on scales of black onyx, each a
ceramic ellipses edged with lead, woven to a gloss.

Nudge of bare heels and both are gone in a fever of mirth; pressure, just a
touch, one side or the other, then its left or right, a yaw across the still
waking light. A lean back and both soar to where eagles fear to climb; a
look down and in peels of outrageous, uproarious laughter they dive
singing through the earth's bedrock… and it flies the lad to where the
earth spirits swim…

… this boy
and the dragon energies he's tamed

… whisperer of the wildest places.

Circuit Boards

I'm an alien

borrowing someone else's time zone, thank you for the loan, where everything seems to run like clockwork.

I'm looking down on the cityscape you show me, ring roads bypassing streets and canals in urban greenfield, emerald set in darker malachite. A circuit board's suburbia of thoroughfares leading to everywhere; and everywhere someone's somewhere bright as solder with every home set in its own cul-de-sac.

You hold out the future
spread across the palms of your hands. Here's tomorrow's world for yesterday's man, all mapped out with high rise images, capacitors for skyscrapers, inductors, resisters, they'll do for other buildings in my map reading across transformers transforming the way I see things, and with you showing me the way to go.

You are my GPS
to another paradigm, the lad with a screw driver disassembling a yesterday's three-in-one, and cassette player.

'What's that grandad?'

What indeed, old history, that's what that is; once cutting edge, an idea as old as magnetic tape.

I follow those little printed avenues through their high-tech parks, formally planted with diodes and sensors, all tended by an invisible army of urban gardeners, all watched over by the micro controller.

Tomorrow's world and a little bit of
yesterday-be-gone lying in
the opened palms of tomorrow's child.

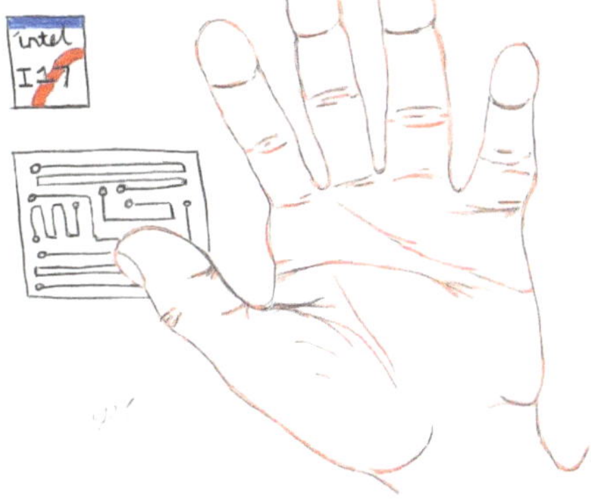

Deft Hands

Deft fingers digitise the crinkle of paper folding small hands along the leading edges of delta-winged fantasies. Deffo-supersonic sellotape achieves flight's brief window that the limits of physics has only ever dreamed of... but you can't beat bedroom limitations.

The brick and mortar barrier,
the thud barrier,
the new nose-cone barrier,
or a gypsum studding wall.

But there's always spare room moon base, that's somewhere to think about for your visiting alien.

Tomorrow we'll voyage to the bottom of the sea in a cardboard and masking tape submarine past pods of whales and shoals of plesiosaurs, oceans rich in plasma... blood for the soul.

Wings my boy!!
You'll be able to fly anywhere in the universe with them and not even have to leave your bedroom. While outside rain stops play as the last day of winter rips a hole through spring and indoors supersonic speeds achieve the bedroom impossible made possible

... probable...

... maybe-ble...

... could-be-ble...

and of course-able there's always tomorrow-ble's make believe-ables.

Delish—Calculi

Chocolate buttons count out a multi-coloured, varied, sugar-coated confectionary... popular brand name, trade mark registered... by-the-by.

The math spreads out a fresh tablecloth, waits to matriculate an hour's calculus, while the edible alternative to the abacus is studied with some misgivings...

'They're not all there!' pricked the bubble of quiet between us... the silence pregnant with suspense had been delivered of surprise—in triplicate... never misses a thing this boy; he eyeballed me suspiciously;

'Pappous, you've been eating them!' Opening gambit by the prosecuting counsel. You will notice that there is no space for any benefit of the doubt in this statement—and he's not giving an inch.

'Pappous, how am I supposed to add and times if you keep taking away?' Playing to the jury, even if he did have point.

'Minus—subtraction? replying for the defence didn't work.

When you're caught, your caught,
Smartie-pants!

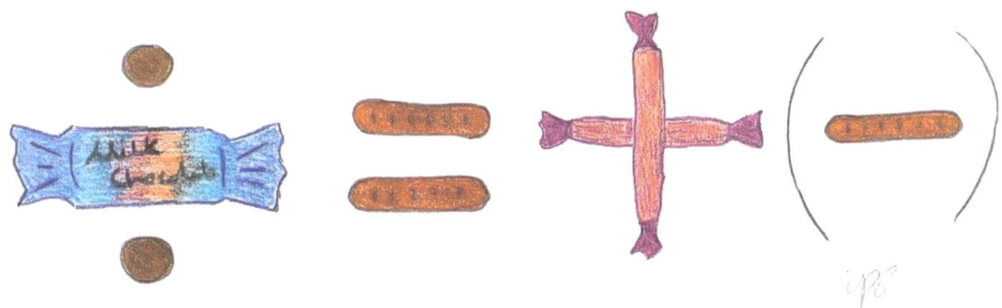

Each Time You Return to Me Someone New

Each time you return to me someone new and the day will come when you shall barely recognise the boy you are now.

Childhood games keeping us in play… the mental pictures treasuring us through their sepia fade, which shall bleach to a whisper of who we are in the moment.

Each parting takes us one step further away from our Magic Kingdom… this slow shedding of youth as we both grow, I greying, you to where wisdom seeks you out for her fertile futures

…tomorrow's bequest, your inheritance,

Grandson…

Fun Day Out

Portmeirion, Summer 2016

It's the calm after the storm, the tide subsides on the crest of a wave and
takes with it the last over-excited squeal of joy through gates now closing.
Air sticky with candy floss; sun super-sweet cold shouldering colder
shadows. Lawns inviolate, gone what eyes who would have ignored *keep off
the grass* signs had there been any. Wrappers litter the breeze whipping up
a flutter of jack staffs, evening flies the flag, halyards tinker with the hollow
ring of masts. Gates close, the place sighs, the fun leaves by the front door
except for a last parental marshalling, defiance a final disobedience...

...come here now...

       ...don't do that...

              ...now where are you off to...

...no, you can't have another ice cream;
       do you see the stand still open?
         Well then!

In the thrall of a toy boat a small boy has his course charted; home, a bath
set to sail a soapy sea. Storm's finally blown out, excitement subsides,
softens the sea into reflection again.

Gilt Edged Invitation

It's the Nobel Prize for Everything-s.

Pulitzer for Grandma's Butter Tablet Recipe.

Peerage, Knighthood, Order Of Merit rolled into an ice cream cone cornucopia.

Order of the Companion Of Honour for Teddy CH.

Audience with the Pope,

and the kind of invitation only a fool would refuse, such requests for the pleasure of, number less than a handful in the full hand's breadth of a lifetime.

'Will you play with me again tomorrow?' the three-year-old asks on his totter up to bath and bed, and this in a world where there's no such thing as magic, or so grown-ups like to say… who don't know that much anyway.

Its all limited to the limitation of the imagination and, since that is limitless, prepare yourself for tomorrow and be prepared to be anything!

A king,
or queen;

a tiger,
or a tree;

a spaceman,

or a loaf of bread even.

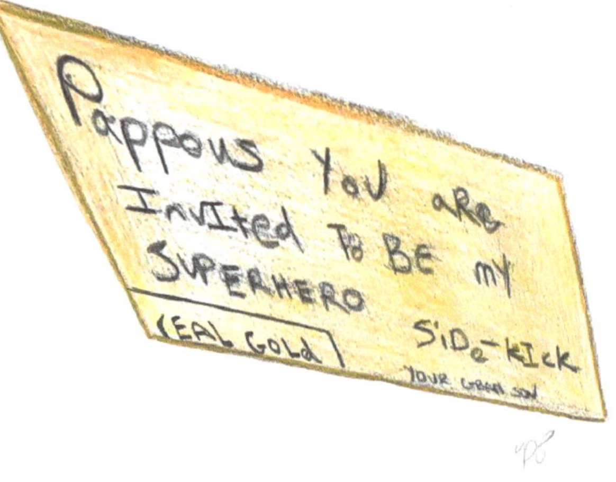

Now the Fun's Gone Home

Garden's grown a bigger place, now the fun's gone home, the greens are less hurried while the leaf-shade shelves the quiet, leading its many voices towards the twilight;

a stillness to dip one's toes into

… not so cold.

All of which I wish I could enrapture, chase down, butterfly net and capture, then pin those gossamer winged joys to a card above a mix of pronunciations in Gothic italics, Indian inking a Latin or Greek mock science name to. This in infectiously irresistible cure to ageing

… nectar of the Gods.

Paper Planes

Life's on the glide,
smooth;

yeah, so smoothly flight squadrons the breakfast table paper chase, slide slipping the hungry space and busiest time for early morning departures.

A yawn deflates, stifled in surprise, as finger four formations peel off their shadow etched flight plans cruising across the wall.

Soft landings rest nonchalantly, leaning so easy cool on one wing.

Pilot's refuelling,
the stratosphere must wait, though time doesn't like to... small fingers busy the toast, mach five and counting.

'Don't bolt your food!'

Pooh Sticks

for Aiden

Two figures stand on a bridge and challenge the waters flowing beneath them. While neither can quite remember which stick belonged to whom the younger maintains his had always won.

Argument would have been a fruitless pursuit.
The afternoon was about more than that.
The point had been to play the game.

One learns to be a good loser.

The only real winner was the river.

Will the little boy cherish the day for as long as his companion, even when it is time for the elder to be called home from The Hundred Acre Wood?

Rhetorical Moment

What is
Inter-molecular structure?
The seven-year-old asked me... with him knowing the answer it became a trick question... youth putting age on the back foot.

Well,
um... err...
humph...

... you know, I like the ring of those words of his and the boy soprano voice which asked them... they have a musical quality which seems to speak in a language I have yet to master.

If mathematics is a language, then does it follow that this question is the poetry of science?

He did explain it all,
and I became molecularly informed in words simple enough for a grandfather to understand... of course it goes without saying that the advantage remains his.

Sparrows at the Breakfast Table

Giggle flight's bright and agile shorthand, sudden staccato recited off at lightning speed... didn't get a word of that, or the rest, or what anyone else was saying.

Brittle table top conversation made all the more fragile by the concrete, steel, and glass, and the shrill stammer of chairs dragging alloy across raw tile.

Sparrows playing with us, grabbing at crumbs of shared communication, the words falling from our tables. A dash in, then off, with something someone had just said, to the far corner of the breakfast time.

All in good fun, their spritely gait, pirouettes, and ducking dives which made us hurry to finish what we were saying between mouthfuls.

Empty chairs at an adjacent table become a moment's perch. We were kept under close observation, no secrets here, as they hang onto every crumb of what we said... rich pickings, snippets of gossip

... cool runnings,

then smart sharp exit as the boy takes flight, dashes out, seizes the sun with both hands, makes the morning his flight of fancy

and runs with it.

Stamping Ground

Go on,
off you go;
march in time to the rat-tat-tat the drummer boy tattoos… boots on the
ground, the seven-year itch stamping out a summerhood's frustration and
the bits of plastic building brick that won't quite fit,

but nearly,
so nearly do,
just not nearly enough.

If this was the sum of all our problems we'd be in clover,

hunger,
homelessness,
child neglect

looked back on as something belonging to somewhere long ago… when
wars would be a cautionary tale about how not to behave… and being sorry
really an acceptance of forgiveness.

But only
if we could build a world
—out of plastic bricks even—
worthy of every seven-year-old… everyone a have,
and poverty had by no one

… and a byword for history.

Summer Time

The small hands of a child sever a dandelion stem, steal a few moments from an unkempt patch of wild ground. Time left to go to seed now told in a few short breaths. This was where we too used to turn the heads of grasses into carronades and fight pitched battles among the clouds of pollen, our war-cries raucous childhood laughter.

Our younger conscripts still refight those old conflicts with all the rough and tumble, and vigour, the younger than tens can muster. Though it must be said that not all clocks tell the same time; as a single weighty gust has a handful of dandelion heads tell us that tea time is still only one o'clock.

The Geology of Beach Pebbles

I had a vantage point in the wings of spring. May well on the wane, June in waiting and weeks to go before the flailing sun would rage. From my corner on the cusp of summer I observed something like a water colour of life take shape.

A mother and her young son walked the shingle to the water's edge where they sat and counted beach pebbles. Trading size, colour, texture of sea-smoothed stone while she chatted with her friend who had come and joined in the harvest.

The wind ruffled their words, scrambling confidences, I heard voices though their diction was indistinct. His play at the fringes of their conversation traced the white lines mapping vein stones, a finger tip's feel over welts and bruises setting tone to the colour.

For a backdrop swash and uprush of breakers fumbling in to trip over their own backwash, rattle of pebbles jingling a chatter-echo against quiet words the gusting shielded. White horses hoofed the shallows, Beaufort Scale coursing in.

It was only a stone's throw, still they maintained a polite distance from an ageless tale of adultery with their backs set to this affair. Youth very much on her side, love on his, and they clutched at the straws of a lusting childish kind of love. So conspicuous the averted gazes, while in fascination I was enveloped, drawn a little jealously into their uncharted beachside ballet.

Mother, friend and child beat the late afternoon chill, sun glinting, bristling through the breeze's clenched teeth of steel, as they walked the shingle back up to my vantage point at the beachside café.

Love lingered in this cold corner of late spring. The couple left played alone at the water's edge. Till the picture's last detail sank into dusk's now empty beach. Its seaside café closing up for the day, a small boy who walked away having palmed a pebble of sunshine salvaged from his day's waning joys,

In this final dab of colour.

This Boy Was Born to Run

This boy trains dragons, stables dinosaurs in his pocket, surely he can tease the breeze and tickle it like a trout.

This boy who ran and ran

barefoot through a fresh cut of summer grass. In his hand the wind he has tamed and tied to a kite's tail, always a whisker short of flight, till overwhelmed, it let its cargo fall before collapsing exhausted at his feet.

He would not let go, though.

Those childish limbs running, small feet scything on the cusp of a sprint. Chivying up the excitement, but the expired breeze dead to encouragement. Brute force had broken the fresh morning spell, charmed by chill, even before sun coming to the rescue had the clouds part company

and summer blue swallow the sky whole.

Now this boy, he too stops to catch his breath… and elevenses.

Tomorrow's World

Crouched over tomorrow's world a teddy's hug kneels in the ripple-surf of an unmade bed, the linen lapping at your knees.

A hundred million galaxies at your fingertips, knowledge of the ancients, quantum tomorrow's physics in animation

… and the caricature of our animated yester-childhoods, cartoon reruns, reunions outrun by CGI, acetates museum pieces… your tomorrow a mouse-click virtual reality

… virtually tomorrow,

and then tomorrow's tomorrow,

and then?

Sky's the limit.

What Each Visit Leaves Behind

Each visit leaves behind an outbox of the elfin child's memes… a pixel print file sharing a clumsy trip over a 'guess what' vocabulary, words the size of gardens for such a young voice… tumble of joys.

I knew a boy like him once, a forever ago it seems now, and at a time when to photo-shop was decades off-line… dream on Flash Gordon,

whose in-box brought today's man all stubbly and laughter serious… shy smiles remembering playdays marshalling G I Joes by the regiment

… son!

Wonder

The sandman used to waylay evenings, the Achilles Heel hamstringing tired eyes into fending off sleep, just for those few minutes more… Please, Mum. Exhaustion the foe as with itching stare, eyes peeled staring out at the lights of the town across the bay, becoming somewhere suddenly exotic.

Bed could wait but never did.

Now the small person in the adult on infrequent nights and at the same window reclaims the apparent lack of change. Landmarks searched out intently till breath steams against the glass and once again obscures then daytime place names street lights mark.

Just as all those years ago a clear night can still draw a latent childhood gaze skyward into the legends of The Man In The Moon.

Just imagine someone one day going to visit him.